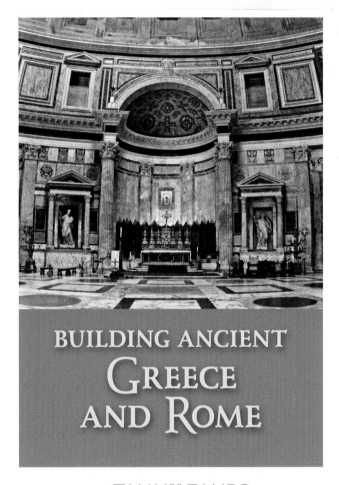

BUILDING ANCIENT
GREECE
AND ROME

BY TAMMY ZAMBO

Editorial Offices: Glenview, Illinois • Parsippany, New Jersey • New York, New York

Sales Offices: Needham, Massachusetts • Duluth, Georgia • Glenview, Illinois Coppell, Texas • Ontario, California • Mesa, Arizona

The Influence of Ancient Greece and Rome

The ancient Greeks and Romans lived more than two thousand years ago, in lands many thousands of miles from the United States. Yet even today, our form of government is a **democracy**, or a government by the people. Democracy is an idea first developed in ancient Greece. In addition, many modern languages are based on Latin, the language that was used in ancient Rome.

The lasting influence of ancient Greece and Rome can also be seen in the **architecture** of buildings throughout the United States and other countries. Architecture is the art and science of designing and erecting buildings. The way people lived in ancient Greece and Rome shaped their architecture. In turn, their architecture shaped the way they lived.

Columns and Capitals

Many buildings in ancient Greece and Rome featured tall columns that decorated and helped support the structures. Many columns were fluted, or carved with decorative vertical lines. At the top of every column was a part called a *capital*. There were three orders, or styles, of capitals.

The Doric order was simple, with thick columns and undecorated capitals.

The Ionic order was more elegant, with thinner columns and curl-shaped decorations on the capitals.

The Corinthian order, more popular with the Romans than with the Greeks, was even fancier, with capitals decorated with a leafy pattern.

2

The Temples of Ancient Greece

The ancient Greeks worshipped many gods and goddesses. They built and dedicated a separate temple to each one. The most important temple in the city of Athens was the Parthenon. It was positioned prominently on the Acropolis, the highest hill in the city, where many temples and related buildings were located. The Parthenon was dedicated to Athena, the goddess of war, wisdom, and crafts. Athena was also considered to be the guardian of Athens, and it is for her the city is named.

Greek temples were not places for worship like today's churches, synagogues, or mosques. Instead, each temple was considered to be a "house" for the god or goddess to whom it was dedicated. People went to a temple only occasionally, to ask a particular god or goddess for protection or favor, or on festival days. They might also leave a small token or offering of food at an altar as a gift.

The Parthenon was built between 447
and about 432 B.C.

A House for Athena

The architecture of the Parthenon reflects the idea that the temples were houses for the gods. The outer part of the temple consisted of a "porch" with an impressive Doric marble *colonnade*, or row of columns, around all four sides. Inside this colonnade, a shorter row of columns appeared at each end of the temple. Next was an inner chamber called a *cella* (SEL-eh) made of stone blocks with an entrance at each end. The *cella* was divided into two rooms. The main room featured a wooden statue of Athena that stood 40 feet (12 meters) high and was covered with more than a ton of ivory and gold. The smaller room, in the rear of the temple, was a treasury that housed other statues, jewels, and vases paid as tribute to Athens by the Delian League.

The Parthenon was also the center of a yearly summer festival honoring Athena, called the Panathenaea (pan-AH-thee-NAH-ay-ah). This was the city's largest festival, and most of the people in the city took part in it. Every four years the celebration became even grander, attracting residents of city-states all around Athens as well.

One major part of the festival involved an enormous procession of people and animals from the largest city gate through the streets of Athens and up to the Acropolis and the Parthenon. The Greeks designed the Acropolis with a lot of open space around the Parthenon so that large crowds like these could conduct their sacred rituals outside without disturbing the gods and goddesses inside the temples.

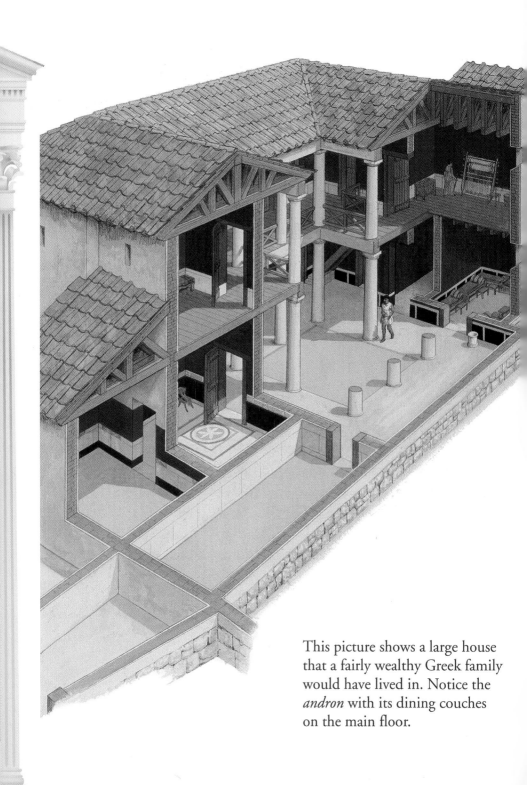

This picture shows a large house that a fairly wealthy Greek family would have lived in. Notice the *andron* with its dining couches on the main floor.

A Greek House

Houses of the ancient Greeks were built in all sizes. They typically would feature a central courtyard with rooms on at least three sides. Some houses had an upper floor of rooms as well. The rooms usually had only small open windows with wooden shutters, because the Greeks valued their privacy. Baked clay tiles covered the roof, allowing rainwater to fall evenly from them.

The houses were designed so that the courtyard was shaded and cool during the many hot months of the year. The courtyard was a gathering place for the family. The house also had an indoor altar, where the family would pray daily and present offerings to the gods and goddesses.

If a house was large enough, certain rooms (usually upstairs) were used only by women, and others (usually downstairs) were used by men. One of the men's rooms was the *andron*, or dining room, where the man of the house would entertain male guests. Because the Greeks ate while reclining, they often used dining couches rather than chairs. The *andron* was designed with a low platform around the edges to hold several dining couches.

The Greek Theater

One of the ancient Greeks' lasting contributions to later civilizations, including ours, was the theater. The first plays were performed in the **agora**, the outdoor marketplace and center of Athenian government. As plays became more popular and more people attended, performances were moved to a part of Athens next to the Acropolis, where one slope of  the hill formed a kind of auditorium. The audience sat on this slope in wooden seats and looked down on a central area that became the stage. In time, these seats were made out of stone, and a wooden framework behind the stage was also erected. Scenery could be attached to the framework, and actors could climb onto the roof for certain scenes.

The most famous Greek playwrights, or writers of plays, were Aeschylus (ES-kih-lehs), Sophocles (SOF-uh-kleez), and Euripedes (yoo-RIP-eh-deez). Many of their plays were somewhat like modern-day musicals, because they included a chorus of twelve to fifteen men. All of the roles in a play, including female roles, were played by men.

An Improved Material

The ancient Romans used many of the Greeks' building designs in their architecture, such as the basic design of Greek temples. Creative **innovations** in building materials, however, allowed the Romans to construct new designs as well.

The Pantheon in Rome was a temple dedicated to all the gods and goddesses. Like Greek temples, it was built with a porch supported by columns. Its *cella*, however, was round instead of rectangular, with a massive dome. This was a new development in architecture.

The Romans were able to build domes like the one in the Pantheon because of a new building material: concrete. Greek materials had been limited to wood, different types of stone, brick, and marble. The Romans figured out how to mix stone or brick with water, lime, and volcanic earth. The product, concrete, was much stronger than other materials. Using concrete, the Romans built stronger arches and curved roofs called *vaults*. They combined these techniques in a dramatic way to build the round *cella* and dome of the Pantheon.

The Pantheon was built between A.D. 118 and 125.

Roman Living Quarters

A house in ancient Rome was called a *domus* (DOM-uhs). Only a wealthy family could afford to live in a *domus*. The center of the domus was the *atrium* (AY-tree-uhm), or hall, with an opening in the ceiling over a small pool. Usually the atrium also held a *lararium* (lah-RAHR-ee-uhm), a shrine dedicated to the household gods. Around the atrium were arranged the dining room, the kitchen, and a study. Bedrooms were located either off the atrium or upstairs, if the *domus* had a second level. Rooms next to the street were often rented out as

This is a picture of a *domus*.

shops. In the back of the *domus* was an open-air garden surrounded by a colonnade called a *peristyle* (PEHR-ih-stile). The walls of a *domus* were often painted, and the floors might be decorated with beautiful mosaics, or pictures made of small colored tiles.

Most Romans lived in crowded apartment buildings, called *insulae* (IN-seh-lee). Many *insulae* were several stories high and poorly built, with a wooden frame and floor. Fires in *insulae* were common, so laws were passed limiting the number of floors an *insula* could have.

Roman Religion

The Romans borrowed most of their deities from the Greeks but gave them new names. Zeus, the king of the Greek gods, was called Jupiter. Hera, Zeus' wife and the protector of families and the home, became Juno. Just as the people of Athens specially honored the goddess Athena, Romans worshipped the goddess Roma.

During the Roman Empire, in addition to worshipping these gods and goddesses, Romans worshipped their **emperor**. Romans also believed that their ancestors' spirits watched over their homes and families. These spirits were called *lares* (lahr-EEZ). Other household gods were called *penates* (peh-NAY-teez), and watched over a family's food. The *lares* and *penates* were worshipped within each home in a special place called a shrine.

As the empire expanded, Romans came into contact with people of other cultures. In time, some Romans adopted the belief systems of those cultures, including Judaism and Christianity.

The Roman Water System

One of the innovations the Romans are best known for is their system of running water. Using their improved arches and new vaults, they built aqueducts, which were raised structures with channels for the movement of water from mountain springs and rivers to the cities. The aqueducts were designed so that gravity kept water flowing through them. Once it reached the city, the water was collected in enormous tanks called *castella*. From the *castella*, a maze of lead pipes then carried water to public buildings and to some private houses.

Most people did not have toilets in their houses or apartments, so they would go to a latrine, or a public toilet. Some of these latrines were in bathhouses. Bathhouses met many other needs as well. They were places to exercise, bathe, get a massage, snack, and relax. Some even included a library. The well-planned design of the baths included a heating system so that a visitor could bathe in separate hot, lukewarm, and cold pools.

The Romans' drainage system was equally well designed. A network of drains under the streets took away waste water and sewage. Many latrines were flushed with water that had already been used in public fountains or bathhouses. You could say that the Romans recycled their water in this way.

The Romans built this aqueduct near Tarragona, Rome's earliest important settlement in Spain. The aqueduct was built in the first century B.C. and was once part of the water supply network for the city.

The Circus Maximus

Another popular Roman activity was attending chariot races at an enormous racetrack called the Circus Maximus. A full day's program included twenty-four races. The circus could also be used for foot races, trick-riding shows on horseback, and games involving **gladiators**.

In the center of the Circus Maximus was a long, low structure called the *spina* (SPY-nah). It was decorated with statues, trophies, and a row of large movable egg- or dolphin-shaped counters. One of these counters was turned over at the start of each lap in a race.

Built into one end of the oval racetrack were twelve starting gates. At the start of a race, each gate would spring open and a team of two, four, or even ten horses would charge forward, pulling a chariot with one driver, called a charioteer. The teams would race seven laps counterclockwise around the *spina*. Chariot races were dangerous, and teams risked crashing into each other. Charioteers were often killed or injured in such collisions.

The Circus Maximus could seat hundreds of thousands of people. As in a stadium like the Colosseum, the seats rose in staircase fashion around the track. Vaulted areas below the seats supported the structure, and audience members climbed stairways in these areas to reach the higher seats. The Roman senators sat in the stone seats closest to the track. The poorest spectators stood high above the track in the area farthest from the action. The emperor and other important public figures sat in a special "boxed seat" decorated with columns like a small temple.

Achievements in Architecture

The ancient Greeks and Romans used great skill and imagination in their architecture. Both the Parthenon and the Pantheon display how they honored their gods and goddesses. Their houses were often built around a courtyard or a hall with an opening in the roof.

The Greeks' achievements in architecture include the Parthenon and their houses. While the Romans borrowed much of their architecture from the Greeks, they developed their own innovations. The Romans used concrete to build domed structures. They also built aqueducts and outdoor racetracks. The way the Greeks and Romans lived can be seen in the way they built structures.

The Circus Maximus was built in the sixth century B.C. Many emperors, including Caligula and Nero, were great fans of the chariot races.

Glossary

agora the outdoor marketplace and center of government in Athens

architecture the art and science of designing and erecting buildings

democracy a government by the people

emperor the ruler of an empire

gladiator a professional Roman fighter

innovation something newly introduced